ESSENTIAL ELEMENTS

FOR BAND

COMPREHENSIVE BAND METHOD

TIM LAUTZENHEISER

JOHN HIGGINS

CHARLES MENGHINI

PAUL LAVENDER

TOM C. RHODES

DON BIERSCHENK

Student Activation Code
E2BT-7214-4639-5544

ISBN 0-634-01298-3

HAL•LEONARD®
CORPORATION
7777 W. BLUEMOUND RD. P.O. BOX 13819 MILWAUKEE, WI 53213

REVIEW

KEY SIGNATURES

Key of F   Key of G

TIME SIGNATURES

3/4   C

B♭   F#   B♭

Dotted Half Note

Dotted Quarter & Eighth Notes

1st & 2nd ENDINGS

1.   2.

DYNAMICS

p – mf – f

PICK-UP NOTES

TEMPO MARKINGS

Andante
Maestoso

6. AMERICA/GOD SAVE THE QUEEN

Andante

Based on a Traditional Anthem

p

7. WEARING OF THE GREEN

Moderato

Irish Folk Song

mf

8. ROSES FROM THE SOUTH

Allegro

Johann Strauss, Jr.

f   *p*   *f*

1.   2.

p

9. CRUISIN' THROUGH THE PARK

Moderato

mf

1.   2.

10. TRUMPET VOLUNTARY — Duet

Jeremiah Clarke

Maestoso

1.   2.

A

f

B

f

REVIEW

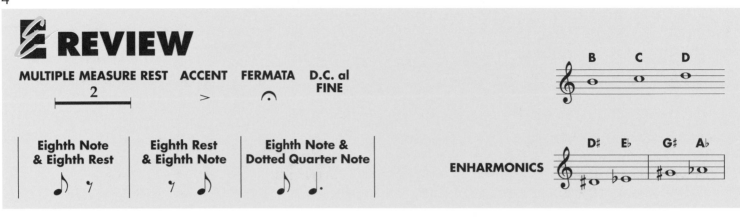

11. CHROMA-ZONE

12. BILLY BOY

American Folk Song

13. TECHNIQUE TRAX

14. SALSA SIESTA – Duet

Staccato

Staccato notes are played lightly and with separation.
They are marked with a dot above or below the note.

15. TREADING LIGHTLY

Tenuto

Tenuto notes are played smoothly and connected, holding each note until the next is played. They are marked with a straight line above or below the note.

16. SMOOTH MOVE

17. SHIFTING GEARS

HISTORY

English composer **Thomas Tallis** (1508–1585) served as a royal court composer for Kings Henry VIII and Edward VI, and Queens Mary and Elizabeth. During Tallis' lifetime, the artist Michaelangelo painted the Sistine Chapel.

Canons (one or more parts imitating the first part) were used in many forms by 16th century composers. A **Round** is a strict (or exact) canon which can be repeated any number of times without stopping. Play *Tallis Canon* as a 4-part round.

18. TALLIS CANON (Round)

Thomas Tallis

Sightreading

Sightreading means playing a musical piece for the first time. The key to sightreading success is to know what to look for *before* you play. Use the word **S-T-A-R-S** to remind yourself what to look for, and eventually your band will become sightreading STARS!

- **S** — **Sharps or flats** in the key signature
- **T** — **Time signature** and **tempo markings**
- **A** — **Accidentals** not found in the key signature
- **R** — **Rhythms**, silently counting the more difficult notes and rests
- **S** — **Signs**, including dynamics, articulations, repeats and endings

19. SIGHTREADING CHALLENGE

DAILY WARM-UPS

WORK-OUTS FOR TONE & TECHNIQUE

20. TONE BUILDER

21. FLEXIBILITY STUDY

22. TECHNIQUE TRAX

23. CHORALE

Johann Sebastian Bach

Andante

24. GRANDFATHER'S CLOCK

Henry C. Work

Allegro

Ritardando   *ritard.* (or) *rit.* –   Gradually slower

25. GLOW WORM

Paul Lincke

Allegretto ◁ *Usually a little slower than Allegro, and with a lighter style.*

rit. ◁ *Watch your director.*

7

26. ALMA MATER – New Note *Practice long tones on all new notes.* A.C. Weekes, W.M. Smith, H.S. Thompson

7

The Scottish folk song *Loch Lomond* is credited to an anonymous soldier who was imprisoned and awaiting execution. In it he writes of his desire to return home to his family and the breathtaking beauty of Loch (Lake) Lomond, a lake in Scotland. Located in the southern highlands, the lake is almost entirely surrounded by hills. One of these is Ben Lomond, a peak 3,192 feet high. **HISTORY**

27. LOCH LOMOND Scottish Folk Song

Key Changes If a key signature changes during a piece of music, you will usually see a thin double bar line at the **key change**. You may also see natural signs reminding you to "cancel" previous sharps or flats. Keep playing, using the correct notes indicated in the *new* key signature. **THEORY**

28. MOLLY MALONE Irish Folk Song

Dynamics *cresc.* = crescendo (or) / *decresc.* = decrescendo (or)

29. RISE AND FALL

30. NO COMPARISON

31. SIGHTREADING CHALLENGE *Remember the S-T-A-R-S guidelines.*

THEORY

 Time Signature
Cut Time (Alla Breve)

 = **2 beats** per measure
= **Half** note gets one beat

𝅝 = 2 beats
𝅗𝅥 = 1 beat
♩ = ½ beat

32. RHYTHM RAP *Clap the rhythm while counting and tapping.*

1 & 2 & 1 & 2 & 1 & 2 & 1 & 2 & 1 & 2 & 1 & 2 & 1 & 2 & 1 & 2 &

33. A CUT ABOVE

1 & 2 & 1 & 2 & 1 & 2 & 1 & 2 & 1 & 2 & 1 & 2 & 1 & 2 & 1 & 2 &

34. TWO-FOUR YANKEE DOODLE

American Folk Song

35. CUT TIME YANKEE DOODLE

American Folk Song

36. MARIANNE

Jamaican Folk Song

37. THE VICTORS

Louis Elbel

38. ESSENTIAL CREATIVITY *Write this example in cut time 𝄵 before playing.*

Dynamics

mp — *mezzo piano* (moderately soft)

Use full breath support at all dynamic levels.
p — *mp* — *mf* — *f*

39. A - ROVING
Moderato

mp ... *f* ... *mp*

Syncopation

Syncopation occurs when an accent or emphasis is given to a note that is not on a strong beat. This type of "off-beat" feel is common in many popular and classical styles.

THEORY

40. RHYTHM RAP
Clap

1 & 2 & 1 & 2 & 1 & 2 & 1 & 2 & 1 & 2 & 1 & 2 & 1 & 2 & 1 & 2 &

41. IN SYNC

1 & 2 & 1 & 2 & 1 & 2 & 1 & 2 & 1 & 2 & 1 & 2 & 1 & 2 & 1 & 2 &

42. LA ROCA
Puerto Rican Folk Song
Moderato

f ... *mp* ... *f* ... *f*

American composer **George M. Cohan** (1878–1942) was also a popular author, producer, director and performer. He helped develop a popular form of American musical theater now known as musical comedy. He is also considered to be one of the most famous composers of American patriotic songs, earning the Congressional Medal of Honor in 1917 for his song *Over There*. Many of his songs became morale boosters when the United States entered World War I in that same year.

HISTORY

43. ESSENTIAL ELEMENTS QUIZ – YOU'RE A GRAND OLD FLAG
Words and Music by George M. Cohan
March Style

mf ... *mp* ... *cresc.* ... *f* ... *mp*

9

cresc. ... *f* ... *mp*

THEORY

New Key Signature

This key signature indicates your **Key of D** (Concert C).
Play all F's as F-sharp and all C's as C-sharp.

44. KEY MOMENT – New Note

45. THE MINSTREL BOY

Irish Folk Song

46. CLOSE CALL – New Note

47. VICTORY MARCH

M. J. Shea

THEORY

Cut Time Syncopation

Compare the notation of the melody below with *Victory March* above. Should they sound the same?

48. WINNING STREAK

M. J. Shea

49. SIGHTREADING CHALLENGE *Remember the S-T-A-R-S guidelines.*

Sixteenth Notes

4 sixteenth notes = 1 Beat
Each sixteenth note = ¼ Beat

A single sixteenth note has 2 flags on the stem.

50. RHYTHM RAP

51. SIXTEENTH NOTE FANFARE

52. MOVING ALONG

53. BACK AND FORTH – Duet

54. COMIN' ROUND THE MOUNTAIN VARIATIONS

American Folk Song

55. ESSENTIAL ELEMENTS QUIZ

PERFORMANCE SPOTLIGHT

56. WARM-UP CHORALE

J. S. Bach/Arr. by John Higgins

57. THE THUNDERER – Band Arrangement

John Philip Sousa
Arr. by John Higgins

Reproduced by Permission of Boosey & Hawkes Music Publishers Ltd.

58. HILL AND GULLY RIDER – Band Arrangement

Jamaican Folk Song
Arr. by John Higgins

59. SHENANDOAH – Band Arrangement

American Folk Song
Arr. by John Higgins

PERFORMANCE SPOTLIGHT

60. LAS MAÑANITAS – Band Arrangement

Mexican Folk Song
Arr. by John Higgins

61. RONDEAU – Band Arrangement

Jean-Joseph Mouret
Arr. by John Higgins

D.S. al Fine–Go back to the sign (𝄋) and play until **Fine**.

62. ROCK.COM – Encore Band Arrangement

John Higgins

14

63. RHYTHM RAP

64. SIXTEENTH VARIATIONS

65. SEA CHANTEY

66. AMERICAN FANFARE – New Note

Eb

THEORY

New Key Signature   This key signature indicates your **Key of Bb** (Concert Ab). Play all B's as B-flat and all E's as E-flat.

67. SCALE STUDY

Bb Scale

68. BILL BAILEY

Hughie Cannon

Moderato

69. RHYTHM RAP

70. RHYTHM ETUDE

71. BATTLE STATIONS

72. ENGLISH DANCE

73. BIG ROCK CANDY MOUNTAIN

American Folk Song

74. ESSENTIAL ELEMENTS QUIZ

Rallentando   *rall.*   –   Gradually slower (same as ritardando)

75. SIMPLE SONG – Duet

Watch your director

76. LINE DANCE

77. TECHNIQUE TRAX

Keep 16ths steady

78. THE GALWAY PIPER

Irish Reel

79. MANHATTAN BEACH MARCH

John Philip Sousa

80. SIGHTREADING CHALLENGE   *Remember the S-T-A-R-S guidelines.*

DAILY WARM-UPS

WORK-OUTS FOR TONE & TECHNIQUE

87. TONE BUILDER *Play at a very slow tempo.*

88. FLEXIBILITY STUDY

89. TECHNIQUE TRAX

90. CHORALE

Johann Sebastian Bach

Adagio

HISTORY

French composer **Georges Bizet** (1838–1875) entered the Paris Conservatory to study music when he was only ten years old. There he won many awards for voice, piano, organ, and composition. Bizet's best known composition is the opera *Carmen,* which was first performed in 1875. *Carmen* tells the story of a band of Gypsies, soldiers, smugglers, and outlaws. Originally criticized for its realism on stage, it was soon hailed as the most popular French opera ever written.

91. TOREADOR SONG (from CARMEN)

Georges Bizet

Maestoso

92. LA CUMPARSITA

G. Rodriguez

Enharmonics

93. THE YELLOW ROSE OF TEXAS *Check the key signature.*

American Folk Song

94. SCALE STUDY – New Note

F

Until 1974 Australia's official national anthem was *God Save The Queen*. A competition was held in 1973 to compose a new anthem, but none of the entries met with the judges' approval. Finally the government asked the public to vote, choosing from among Australia's 3 most popular patriotic songs. After easily defeating *Waltzing Matilda* and *God Save The Queen*, *Advance Australia Fair* was officially declared the national anthem of Australia on April 19, 1974.

HISTORY

95. ADVANCE AUSTRALIA FAIR

Peter Dodds McCormick

△ Resume previous tempo

96. ESSENTIAL CREATIVITY

Arrange the melody of "America (My Country 'Tis Of Thee)" for your instrument. Write out the first line (6 measures).
Your first note is G. ADD: Key signature—key of G • Time signature—3/4 • Tempo and dynamic markings.

Play the completed line on your instrument to hear your own version.

97. AMERICAN PATROL

Moderato

F. W. Meacham

98. ARIA (from MARRIAGE OF FIGARO)

Moderato

Wolfgang Amadeus Mozart

HISTORY

American composer **John Philip Sousa** (1854–1932) was best known for his brilliant band marches. Sousa wrote 136 marches, including *The Stars and Stripes Forever,* which was declared the official march of the United States of America in 1987.

99. THE STARS AND STRIPES FOREVER

John Philip Sousa

March Tempo

Check rhythm

100. SIGHTREADING CHALLENGE *Remember the S-T-A-R-S guidelines.*

Moderato

$\frac{6}{8}$ Time Signature

$\frac{6}{8}$ = **6 beats** per measure
= **Eighth** note gets one beat

♪ = 1 beat   ♩ = 2 beats
♩. = 3 beats   ♩. = 6 beats

6/8 time is usually played with a slight emphasis on the **1st** and **4th** beats of each measure. This divides the measure into 2 groups of 3 beats each. In faster music, these two primary beats will make the music feel like it's counted "in 2."

101. RHYTHM RAP *Clap the rhythm while counting and tapping.*

102. LAZY DAY

103. ROW YOUR BOAT

104. JOLLY GOOD FELLOW

105. CHANSON — French Folk Song

106. ESSENTIAL ELEMENTS QUIZ – WHEN JOHNNY COMES MARCHING HOME — American Folk Song

22

More Enharmonics

Remember that notes which sound the same but have different letter names are called **enharmonics**. These are some common enharmonics that you'll use in the exercises below.

More Chromatics

The smallest distance between two notes is a half-step, and a scale made up of consecutive half-steps is a **chromatic scale.** These are usually written with **enharmonic** notes—sharps when going up and flats when going down.

107. CHROMATIC SCALE

Practice slowly until you are sure of all the fingerings.

△ F♯ Enharmonic

108. TECHNIQUE TRAX

HISTORY

A **Habañera** is a Cuban dance and song form in slow 2/4 meter. I\t is named after the city of Havana, the capital of Cuba. Made popular in the New World in the early 19th Century, it was later carried over to Spain. There the rhythms of the Habañera were incorporated into many styles of Latin music. One of the most famous Habañeras is heard in Bizet's *Carmen,* written in 1875.

109. HABAÑERA (from CARMEN)

Georges Bizet

110. CHROMATIC CRESCENDO

111. TURKISH MARCH (from THE RUINS OF ATHENS)

Ludwig van Beethoven

Allegretto

112. THE OVERLANDER

Australian Folk Song

Allegro

113. STACCATO STUDY

Moderato

Eb Enharmonic   C# Enharmonic

F# Enharmonic

114. YANKEE DOODLE DANDY

Words and Music by George M. Cohan

Allegro

115. SIGHTREADING CHALLENGE

Remember the **S-T-A-R-S** guidelines:
S – Sharps or flats in the key signature, **T** – Time signature and tempos, **A** – Accidentals, **R** – Rhythm, **S** – Signs

Moderato

Triplets

A **triplet** is a group of **3** notes played in the space of **2**. In $\frac{2}{4}$, $\frac{3}{4}$, or $\frac{4}{4}$ time, an eighth note triplet is spread evenly across one beat.

116. RHYTHM RAP

117. THREE TO GET READY

118. TRIPLET STUDY

119. MARCH (from THE NUTCRACKER) – Duet

Peter I. Tchaikovsky

120. ESSENTIAL ELEMENTS QUIZ – THEME FROM FAUST

Charles Gounod

25

The first known printing of the lyrics and music to **The Marines' Hymn** dates from August 1, 1918. An unknown author is believed to have taken the opening words of the song from the words on the Marine Corps flag, "From the halls of Montezuma to the shores of Tripoli." The music was taken from "Genevieve de Brabant," by the operetta composer Jacques Offenbach.

127. THE MARINES' HYMN

D.S. al Fine

Play until you see the **D.S. al Fine**. Then go back to the sign (%) and play until the word **Fine**. **D.S.** is the abbreviation for **Dal Segno**, or "from the sign," and **Fine** means "the end."

128. D.S. MARCH

Accelerando

accel. – Gradually faster.

129. CAN–CAN

Jacques Offenbach

accel.

△ Watch your director.

130. TARANTELLA

Italian Folk Song

Allegro

The **waltz** is a dance in moderate 3/4 time which developed around 1800 from the Ländler, an Austrian peasant dance. Austrian composer **Johann Strauss, Jr.** (1825–1899) composed over 400 waltzes. These include such famous pieces as *The Blue Danube, Tales From the Vienna Woods* and *Emperor Waltz*.

131. EMPEROR WALTZ

Johann Strauss, Jr.

Andantino ◁ *Tempo between Andante and Moderato.*

Legato Style

legato – Played in a smooth, connected style.

132. ENGLISH DANCE – Duet

Johann Christian Bach

Andante

△ *Smooth, connected*

133. ESSENTIAL ELEMENTS QUIZ – BRITISH GRENADIERS

Traditional

Allegretto

134. NASSAU BOUND

Bahamian Folk Song

Count ► 1 & 2 & 3 & 4 &

135. UNFINISHED SYMPHONY THEME

Franz Schubert

136. RHYTHM STUDY

Measure Repeat ⅟. Repeat the previous measure once for each **Measure Repeat** sign.

137. COUNTRY GARDENS

English Folk Song

138. JOSHUA

African-American Spiritual

Major and Minor

THEORY

The scales you've already learned are called **Major** scales. They all follow the same pattern, with **half-steps** between notes 3–4 and between notes 7–8.

Natural Minor scales follow a different pattern, with **half-steps** between notes 2–3 and 5–6. The **A Minor** scale uses the same key signature as **C Major**.

Another type of minor scale is called **Harmonic Minor**, which adds an accidental to raise the **7th** note by a half-step. Compare the scales on the right.

See page 37 for additional minor scales.

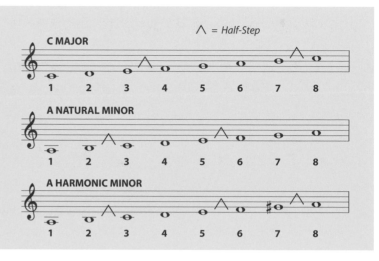

144. NATURAL MINOR SCALE – New Note

145. FINALE FROM "NEW WORLD SYMPHONY"

Antonin Dvořák

146. HARMONIC MINOR SCALE

147. HUNGARIAN DANCE NO. 5

Johannes Brahms

148. POMP AND CIRCUMSTANCE (LAND OF HOPE AND GLORY)

Edward Elgar

PERFORMANCE SPOTLIGHT

D.S. al Coda — Play until you see the **D.S. al Coda**. Then go back to the sign (𝄋) and play until the **Coda Sign** ("To Coda" ⊕). Skip directly to the **Coda** and play until the end.

149. SIMPLE GIFTS – Band Arrangement

Shaker Folk Song
Arr. by John Higgins

150. SEMPER FIDELIS – Band Arrangement

John Philip Sousa
Arr. by John Higgins

PERFORMANCE SPOTLIGHT

151. DANNY BOY – Band Arrangement

Irish Folk Song
Arr. by John Higgins

152. TAKE ME OUT TO THE BALL GAME – Band Arrangement

By Jack Norworth and Harry von Tilzer
Arr. by John Higgins

PERFORMANCE SPOTLIGHT

153. SERENGETI (AFRICAN RHAPSODY) – Band Arrangement

John Higgins

RUBANK® STUDIES

154. CHORALE (Concert B♭)

155. CHORALE (Concert E♭)

156. CHORALE (Concert F)

157. CHORALE (Concert A♭)

158. CHORALE (Concert C)

BARITONE T.C. KEY OF C (CONCERT B♭)

159.

160.

161.

162.

RUBANK® STUDIES

BARITONE T.C. KEY OF F (CONCERT E♭)

163.

164.

165.

166.

BARITONE T.C. KEY OF G (CONCERT F)

167.

168.

169.

170.

RUBANK® STUDIES

BARITONE T.C. KEY OF B♭ (CONCERT A♭)

171.

172.

173.

174.

BARITONE T.C. KEY OF D (CONCERT C)

175.

176.

177.

178.

RUBANK® STUDIES

BARITONE T.C. KEY OF A MINOR (CONCERT G MINOR)

179.

180.

BARITONE T.C. KEY OF D MINOR (CONCERT C MINOR)

181.

182.

BARITONE T.C. KEY OF E MINOR (CONCERT D MINOR)

183.

184.

CHROMATIC SCALES

185.

186.

INDIVIDUAL STUDY – Baritone T.C.

INDIVIDUAL STUDY – Baritone T.C.

193. TONGUING WORK–OUT #2 *CD Track 62*

194. FINGER PATTERNS *CD Track 63*

195. ARTICULATION STUDY #1 *CD Track 64*

196. ARTICULATION STUDY #2 *CD Track 65*

197. ARTICULATION STUDY #3 *CD Track 66*

198. CHROMATIC CHALLENGE *CD Track 67*

INDIVIDUAL STUDY – Baritone T.C.

Solo with Piano Accompaniment

You can perform this solo with the piano accompaniment on the following page.

199. GARNET – Baritone T.C. Solo *CD Track 68*

Vander Cook

INDIVIDUAL STUDY – Baritone T.C.

199. GARNET – Piano Accompaniment *CD Track 69*

Vander Cook

RHYTHM STUDIES

RHYTHM STUDIES

CREATING MUSIC

Theme and Variation

Theme and Variation is a technique used by composers and arrangers to create interesting musical ideas that are "varied" from an established melody, or "theme." Play the following theme and two variations to hear how the arranger has created new phrases based on the original melody.

1. THEME

"Simple Gifts"

VARIATION 1 *Adding some notes • Changing some rhythms*

VARIATION 2 *Removing notes • Changing rhythms • Adding accents • Adding notes*

2. THEME AND YOUR VARIATION

Write your own variation of this theme. Use your instrument to hear and try different ideas.

"Oh, Susanna"

Theme

Your Variation

Blues Improvisation

Improvisation using a **Blues Scale** is an important part of jazz and popular music. Musicians use combinations of these notes and various rhythms to create their own spontaneous solos over a 12 measure progression of chords.

Blues Scale

3. LET'S JAM
Use the indicated notes from the Blues Scale to create your own solo to play with the accompaniment (Line B).

You can mark your progress through the book on this page. Fill in the stars as instructed by your band director.

ESSENTIAL ELEMENTS

STAR ACHIEVER

NAME _____

1. Page 2–4, Review
2. Page 5, Sightreading Challenge, No. 19
3. Page 6, Daily Warm-Ups
4. Page 7, Sightreading Challenge, No. 31
5. Page 8, Essential Creativity, No. 38
6. Page 9, EE Quiz, No. 43
7. Page 10, Sightreading Challenge, No. 49
8. Page 11, EE Quiz, No. 55
9. Page 12–13, Performance Spotlight
10. Page 15, EE Quiz, No. 74
11. Page 16, Sightreading Challenge, No. 80
12. Page 18, Daily Warm-Ups
13. Page 19, Essential Creativity, No. 96
14. Page 20, Sightreading Challenge, No. 100

15. Page 21, EE Quiz, No. 106
16. Page 22, Chromatic Scale, No. 107
17. Page 23, Sightreading Challenge, No. 115
18. Page 24, EE Quiz, No. 120
19. Page 25, EE Quiz, No. 126
20. Page 27, EE Quiz, No. 133
21. Page 30, Natural Minor Scale, No. 144
22. Page 30, Harmonic Minor Scale, No. 146
23. Page 30, Pomp and Circumstance, No. 148
24. Page 31, Performance Spotlight
25. Page 32, Performance Spotlight
26. Page 33, Performance Spotlight
27. Page 38–39, Individual Study
28. Page 40, Performance Spotlight

MUSIC — AN ESSENTIAL ELEMENT OF LIFE

FINGERING CHART

Instrument Care Reminders

Before putting your instrument back in its case after playing, do the following:

- Remove the mouthpiece and wipe it clean. Once a week, wash the mouthpiece with warm tap water. Dry thoroughly.
- Use the water key to empty water from the instrument. Blow air through it.
- Wipe off the instrument with a clean soft cloth. Return the instrument to its case.

Baritone valves occasionally need oiling. To oil your baritone valves:

- Unscrew the valve at the top of the casing.
- Lift the valve half-way out of the casing.
- Apply a few drops of special brass valve oil to the exposed valve.
- Carefully return the valve to its casing. When properly inserted, the top of the valve should easily screw back into place.

Be sure to grease the slides regularly. Your director will recommend special slide grease and valve oil, and will help you apply them when necessary.

CAUTION: If a slide, a valve or your mouthpiece becomes stuck, ask for help from your band director or music dealer. Special tools should be used to prevent damage to your instrument.

○ = Open
● = Pressed down

Instrument courtesy of Yamaha Corporation of America, Band and Orchestral Division

FINGERING CHART

D

D# E♭

E

F

F# G♭

G

G# A♭

A

A# B♭

B

C

C# D♭

D

D# E♭

E

F

F# G♭

G

G# A♭

A

A# B♭

B

C

⚡ REFERENCE INDEX

Definitions (pg.)

A Tempo   19
Accelerando (accel.)   26
Alla Breve   8
Allegretto   6
Andantino   27
Canon   5
Chromatic Scale   22
Chromatics   22
Crescendo (cresc.)   7
Cut Time   8
Cut Time Syncopation   10
D. S. al Coda   31
D. S. al Fine   26
Decrescendo (decresc.)   7
Enharmonics   22
Harmonic Minor Scale   30
Key Change   7
Legato Style   27
Major Scale   30
Marines' Hymn   26
Measure Repeat   28
Mezzo Piano (mp)   9
Natural Minor Scale   30
Rallentando (rall.)   16
Ritardando (rit.)   6
Round   5
Sightreading STARS   5
6/8   21
Sixteenth Notes   11
Solo   40
Staccato   5
Syncopation   9
Tenuto   5
Triplet   24
Waltz   27

Book 1 Review

Accent   4
Allegro   2
Andante   3
Breath Mark   2
D.C. al Fine   4
Dotted Half Note   3
Dotted Quarter Note   3
Dynamics   3
Eighth Note/Rest   2
Enharmonics   4
Fermata   4
1st & 2nd Endings   3
Forte (f)   3
Half Note/Rest   2
Maestoso   3
Mezzo Forte (mf)   3
Moderato   2
Multiple Measure Rest   4
Piano (p)   3
Pick-up Notes   3

Quarter Note/Rest   2
Repeat Sign   2
Slur   2
Tie   2
Time Signature   2, 3
Whole Note/Rest   2

Composers

JOHANN CHRISTIAN BACH
• English Dance   27
JOHANN SEBASTIAN BACH
• Chorale   6
• Chorale   18
LUDWIG VAN BEETHOVEN
• Turkish March (from The Ruins of Athens)   23
GEORGES BIZET
• Toreador Song (from Carmen)   18
• Habañera   22
JOHANNES BRAHMS
• Hungarian Dance No. 5   30
JEREMIAH CLARKE
• Trumpet Voluntary   3
GEORGE M. COHAN
• You're A Grand Old Flag   9
• Yankee Doodle Dandy   23
ANTONIN DVORÁK
• Finale from "New World Symphony"   30
EDWARD ELGAR
• Pomp and Circumstance   30
CHARLES GOUNOD
• Theme from Faust   24
F.W. MEACHAM
• American Patrol   20
JEAN-JOSEPH MOURET
• Rondeau   13
WOLFGANG AMADEUS MOZART
• Aria (from Marriage of Figaro)   20
JACQUES OFFENBACH
• Can-Can   26
G. RODRIGUEZ
• La Cumparsita   19
FRANZ SCHUBERT
• Unfinished Symphony Theme   28
JOHN PHILIP SOUSA
• Manhattan Beach March   16
• Semper Fidelis   31
• The Stars and Stripes Forever   20
• The Thunderer   12
JOHANN STRAUSS, JR.
• Emperor Waltz   27
• Roses From the South   3
THOMAS TALLIS
• Tallis Canon   5
PETER I. TCHAIKOVSKY
• March (from The Nutcracker)   24

World Music

AMERICAN
• Big Rock Candy Mountain   15
• Billy Boy   4
• Comin' Round The Mountain   11
• The Crawdad Song   2
• Joshua   28
• Oh, Susanna   44
• Over the River and Through the Woods   25
• Shenandoah   12
• Shoo Fly   2
• Simple Gifts   31, 44
• When Johnny Comes Marching Home   21
• Yankee Doodle   8
• The Yellow Rose of Texas   19
AUSTRALIAN
• Advance Australia Fair   19
• The Overlander   23
BAHAMIAN
• Nassau Bound   28
ENGLISH
• Country Gardens   28
• Good King Wenceslas   17
• Greensleeves   29
• Shepherd's Hey   2
FRENCH
• Chanson   21
GERMAN
• O Tannenbaum   17
IRISH
• Danny Boy   32
• The Galway Piper   16
• Molly Malone   7
• The Minstrel Boy   10
• Wearing of the Green   3
ITALIAN
• Tarantella   27
JAMAICAN
• Hill and Gully Rider   12
• Marianne   8
MEXICAN
• Las Mañanitas   13
PUERTO RICAN
• La Roca   9
SCOTTISH
• The Blue Bells of Scotland   29
• Loch Lomond   7
THAI
• Thailand Lullaby   2
TRADITIONAL HOLIDAY MUSIC
• Good King Wenceslas   17
• O Tannenbaum   17
• S'Vivon   17